PIANO | VOCAL | GUITAR

PENTATONIX

"Papaoutai" has been omitted from this publication due to licensing restrictions.

ISBN 978-1-4950-1185-6

HAL•LEONARD®
CORPORATION
7777 W. BLUEMOUND RD. P.O. BOX 13819 MILWAUKEE, WI 53213

Visit Hal Leonard Online at
www.halleonard.com

PROBLEM

Words and Music by ILYA, ARIANA GRANDE,
MAX MARTIN, SAVAN KOTECHA
and AMETHYST AMELIA KELLY

6

Additional Lyrics

Rap: Smart money bettin' I'll be better of without you.
In no time I'll be forgettin' all about you.
You saying that you know, but I really really doubt you
Understand my life is easy when I ain't around you.

Mitchy, Mitchy, too biggy to be here stressin',
I'm thinkin' I love the thought of you more than I love your presence.
And the best thing now is prob'ly for you to exit.
I let you go, let you back; I finally learned my lesson.

No half-steppin'. Either you want it or you just playin'.
I'm listening to you, knowin' I can't believe what you're sayin'.
There's a million yous, baby boo, so don't be dumb.
I got ninety-nine problems, but you won't be one, like what?

ON MY WAY HOME

Words and Music by MARCUS LOMAX, CLARENCE COFFEE,
JORDAN JOHNSON, JASON EVIGAN, SAM MARTIN
and STEFAN JOHNSON

LA LA LATCH

Words and Music by AL HAKAM EL KAUBAISY, JAMES MURRAY,
MUSTAFA OMER, SAM SMITH, SHAHID KHAN, JAMES NAPIER,
GUY LAWRENCE, HOWARD LAWRENCE, JONATHAN COFFER
and FROBISHER MBABAZI

RATHER BE

Words and Music by GRACE CHATTO,
JACK PATTERSON, NICOLE MARSHALL
and JAMES NAPIER

SEE THROUGH

Words and Music by KERLI KOIV,
JOONAS ANGERIA and THOMAS KIERJONAN

World un-der__ my skin,__
Stripped down__ to__ my heart,__

there for__ you__ to find.__
na-ked__ to__ the core.__

All I've__ kept__ with-in,__
All of__ me,__ un-chart-

ed,
laid be-fore__ your eyes.__
begs to__ be__ ex-plored.__

I

29

STANDING BY

Words and Music by AVI KAPLAN
and KEVIN OLUSOLA

Where we be - long _____ is side by ___ side. _____

And so we'll hold _____

_____ each oth-er close, _____ and in our souls _____

_____ we're stand-ing ___ by. _____ Ooh, whoa, _